The French Letters

WRITTEN BY
DORGAN RUSHTON

ILLUSTRATED BY
WILLIAM RUSHTON

Rushton Rushton & Rushton
London-Overton

First published in Great Britain 1984

PRINTED IN GREAT BRITAIN
ISBN 0 948082 00 3
Printed by Printfine Limited, Liverpool.

Produced by Paul Rushton

Maidelthorpe

by
G. Ainsley Ffrench
late of
Maidelthorpe
painted aboard the
Ferry-Boat "Victor-Hugo"
from memory,
during the first
stage of the artist's journey
into involuntary Exile.
Farewell, Maidelthorpe.
G. Ainsley Ffrench

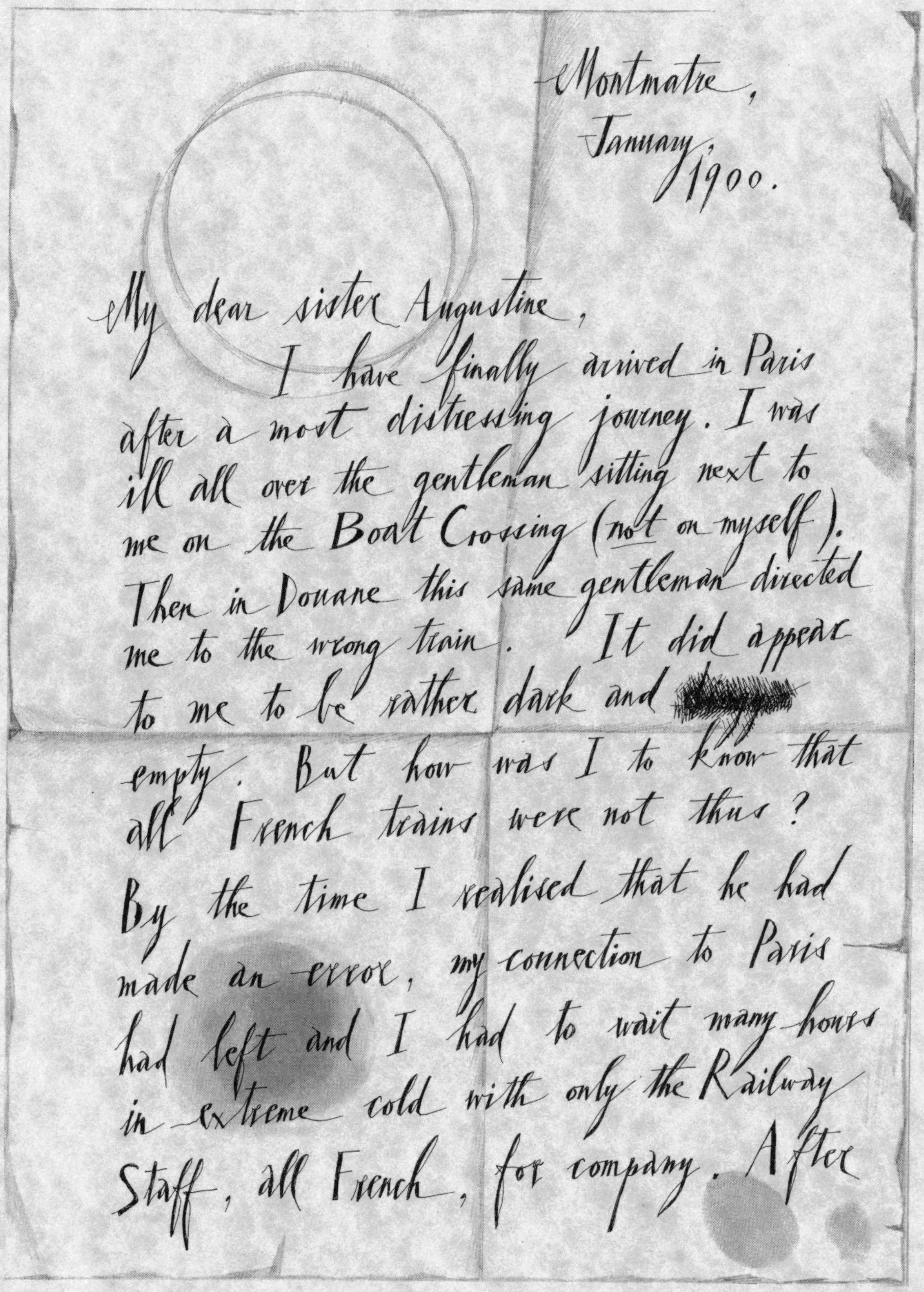

Montmatre,
January,
1900.

My dear sister Augustine,

I have finally arrived in Paris after a most distressing journey. I was ill all over the gentleman sitting next to me on the Boat Crossing (<u>not</u> on myself). Then in Douane this same gentleman directed me to the wrong train. It did appear to me to be rather dark and empty. But how was I to know that all French trains were not thus? By the time I realised that he had made an error, my connection to Paris had left and I had to wait many hours in extreme cold with only the Railway Staff, all French, for company. After

A BEAUTIFULLY PRESERVED SECTION OF A PART OF ONE OF GODWYN FFRENCH'S ORIGINAL LETTERS FROM PARIS.

[The delicate state of these precious papers prevented them from being reproduced in entirity.]

Montmatre,
January.

My dear sister Augustine,

I have finally arrived in Paris after a most distressing journey. I was ill all over the gentleman next to me on the boat crossing (not on myself). Then, in Douane, this same gentleman directed me to the wrong train, which did appear to be rather dark and empty, but how was I to know that all French trains were not thus?

By the time I realized that he had made an error, my connection to Paris had left, and I had to wait many hours in extreme cold with only the railway staff (all French), for company.

After travelling many more hours, I eventually reached my destination, only to learn that the pittance Papa is paying me is far from sufficient to provide respectable lodgings. I have, therefore, been forced by circumstances to move to a seedy slum-area of Paris called Monmarte, where I have taken, for the period of one month only, a most unsavoury garret owned by a Madame Leclerc[1], who is also most unsavoury. I have a small, listing bed, a kitchen chair, a wobbling table, a stove and a great pile of used canvasses, drawing paper and bottles, left, I presume, by the previous tenant.

MESSAGERIES MARITIMES

LE PAQUEBOT NEWHAVEN-DIEPPE

G. Ainsley Ffrench.

Douane, France. 1900.

The bed linen is appalling, and I swear the sheets have been used, but Madame merely shrugs. I enquired of her as to when the floor coverings, drapes and other furnishings would be arriving, only to receive another shrug. She shrugs a good deal.

Sister, I am living in poverty, abject poverty. It is altogether so different from tne Manor at Maidelthorpe that it beggars description. I cannot believe that Papa has cast me out of house and home and banished me to Paris, when he knows I know nothing of the language. He is indeed an heartless man.

For not only do I have to contend with the wretched language, but the money here is completely dissimilar to ours. There are no pounds, shillings and pence, but froncs and other things. The French seem to be greatly excited by the money, and somehow, in the confusion that results when they see banknotes in one's hand, I have been left with none at all, just some various coins to last me for the next five days. It will truly be a miracle if I survive.

If you do not hear from me again, you will know what has befallen me and then, perhaps, Papa will be sorry that he treated me in this beastly

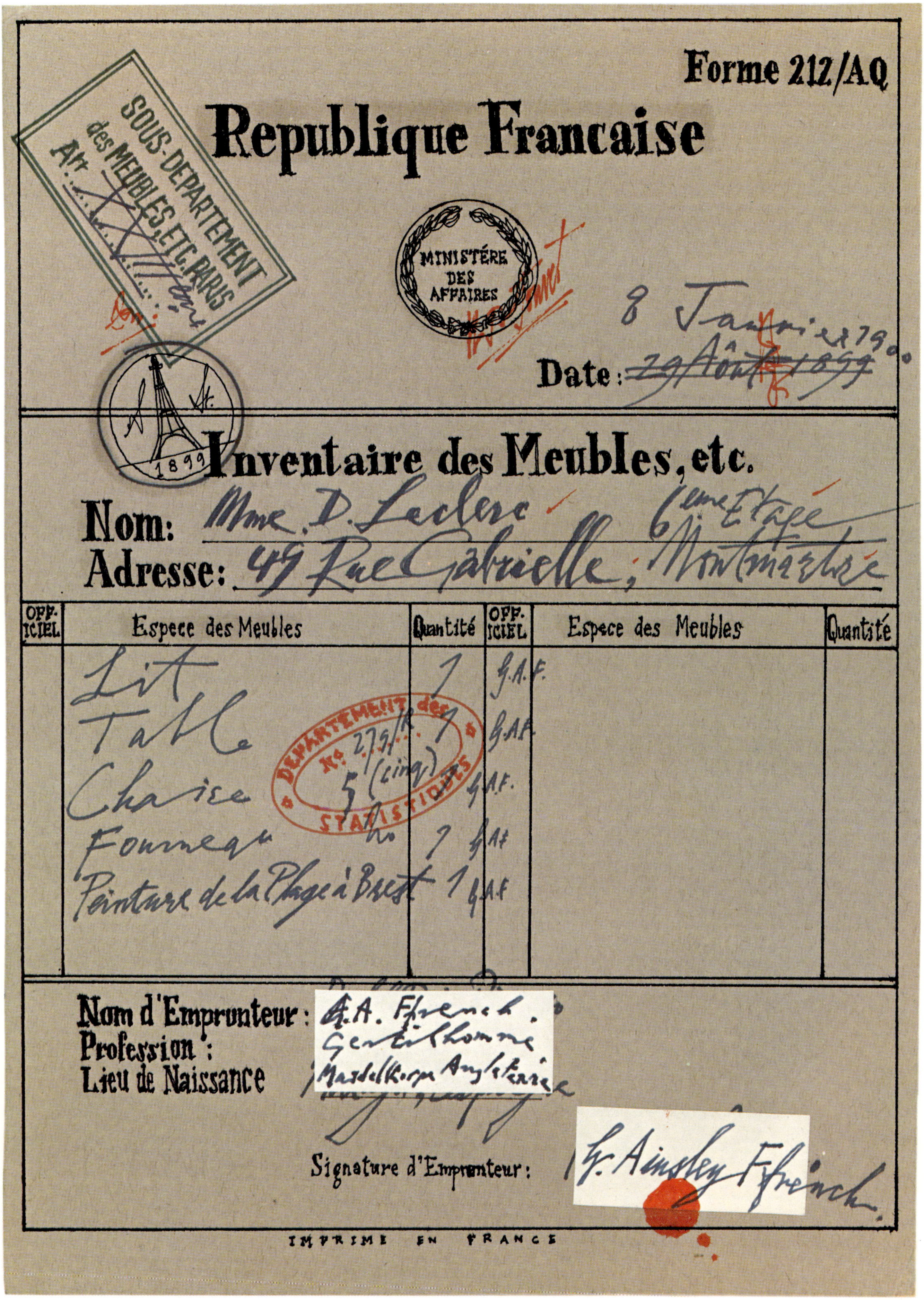

Forme 212/AQ

Republique Francaise

SOUS-DEPARTEMENT des MEUBLES, ETC. PARIS
Arr. XVIII

MINISTÉRE DES AFFAIRES

8 Janvier 1900

Date: ~~29 Août 1899~~

1899

Inventaire des Meubles, etc.

Nom: Mme D. Leclerc   6ème Etage

Adresse: 49 Rue Gabrielle, Montmartre

OFFICIEL	Espece des Meubles	Quantité	OFFICIEL	Espece des Meubles	Quantité
	Lit	1	G.A.F.		
	Table	1	G.A.F.		
	Chaise	5	G.A.F.		
	Fourneau	1	G.A.F.		
	Peinture de la Plage à Brest	1	G.A.F.		

DEPARTEMENT des STATISTIQUES
No. 279/R.
5 (cinq)

Nom d'Emprunteur: G.A. Ffrench.
Profession: Gentilhomme
Lieu de Naissance: Mardelkorpe Angleterre

Signature d'Emprunteur: G. Ainsley Ffrench.

IMPRIME EN FRANCE

fashion. It is manifestly unfair. After all, dear Augustine, you, too, were involved in the incest, and yet he has allowed you to remain on at the Manor. Why should I be the only one to suffer?

I am, without doubt, the most miserable person in the world.

I have only the smallest piece of candle left, and now I see that it has started to snow, so I must to bed before I freeze, or worse. it is after eleven o'clock. I have never been up until this hour in my life. It is no wonder I am tired.

There is a great deal of noise coming from the street below. I am certain it will keep me awake. What can they be doing in the middle of the night? Perhaps, like the money, the hours are different to English hours. But how will I ever know?

I am not sure that I will see the morning.

Your affectionate brother,

Godwyn

P.S. In the event, goodbye.

Monmartre,
February.

Dear sister Augustine,

My allowance is not enough to maintain a rat in Paris. Very soon I may be forced to seek employment of some type, but how I am to succeed in this, when I do not know the French for it, I do not know. Une position?

I am, unfortunately, still residing in this squalid attic and it has been extremely cold. However the previous occupant (clearly an inebriate, to judge from the bottles), left an enormous stack of abominable pictures so I am able to keep warm by burning them. What he will say when he returns I do not know and I do not care particularly, for by then I hope to be in a properly furnished ground floor room in a reputable area.

It is too bad of Papa to have exiled me to Paris. Were I less than eighteen the persons I am compelled to associate with could be of a very damaging influence.

You would never believe the hours they keep here. Last night there was a knocking on my door well past midnight The lady who thus woke me from my slumbers was none other than a Native of Africa, (see Marvels Of The Modern World.[1] On my bookshelf).

CAFÉ · BRASSERIE
Prouets'
BILLARD
101, BOULEVARD DE CLICHÉ
PARIS
G. Ainsley Ffrench.
La Chaise
A mes chers amis
Suzanne et Henri
Picasso
1900

My dear sister, I tell you the following, not to alarm you, but that you may press Papa to send further monies, so that I may move to more suitable surroundings.

Having woken me, the negress showed no shame and laughed aloud at my night attire. Then she proceeded (and I swear this is true, Augustine) to lift her petticoats way above her knees, showing her britches. She kicked her legs in the air and shouted repeatedly that I could. That was all I understood, the rest being in French or maybe African. However, having had incest with a lady living nearby last week, and then finding I had to pay her my whole allowance, I firmly refused the negress's offer and managed to push her away. I slammed and bolted the door, but she is living downstairs, and I live in fear of her catching me and of losing my allowance again.

The food here is horrid. No one has ever heard of porridge.

There are stacks of papers in this attic. I use the ones that are very scribbled on as tapers for the fire (I do not think you are ever likely to hear of P. Ruiz Picassó[2]) and I

take the others, with my paintbox, and go out sketching as we used to do at Maidelthorpe. I am using it to teach myself ~~Ffrench~~ French. Everyone speaks it here. I feel like Robinson Caruso[3]. By the way, he is singing here somewhere, I think. I saw a poster. Is he not the one you admire on Papa's cylinders?

I spend a good deal of the time thinking. I think I should like to go into banking. I think I may when I have the French.

They have started another party downstairs. I expect they are all drinking again. Soon my table will start to shake, so I will end this letter while I am still legible.

Pity me, dear Augustine, living in this wretched place.

Your poor brother,

Godwyn

Montmatre,
March.

Dearest Augustine,

How very difficult it is to make myself understood here, armed only with the French-English Dictionary Papa threw at me as I left the Manor. An English-French Dictionary would have served a much more useful purpose. If your allowance is stretching further than mine dear sister, (as indeed it should), then perhaps you could purchase one for me and send it to me post haste.

I commenced, with the utmost diligence, to work my way alphabetically through Papa's dictionary. I found that 'A' means 'in' and 'by' and 'to' and 'at'. The second word was 'abaissement', which does not mean a basement, as one would think, but humiliation. The very next word was 'abandon' which means abandon. So it does not seem to me to be a very logical language, and as both these last English words pertained so directly to my present predicament, I found it hard not to weep and could go no further with my studies.

I have now invented a new method of learning which has proved far less distressing. I leaf through the dictionary keeping my eyes closed, then mark a word with my thumbnail (which is growing at an alarming rate. I am

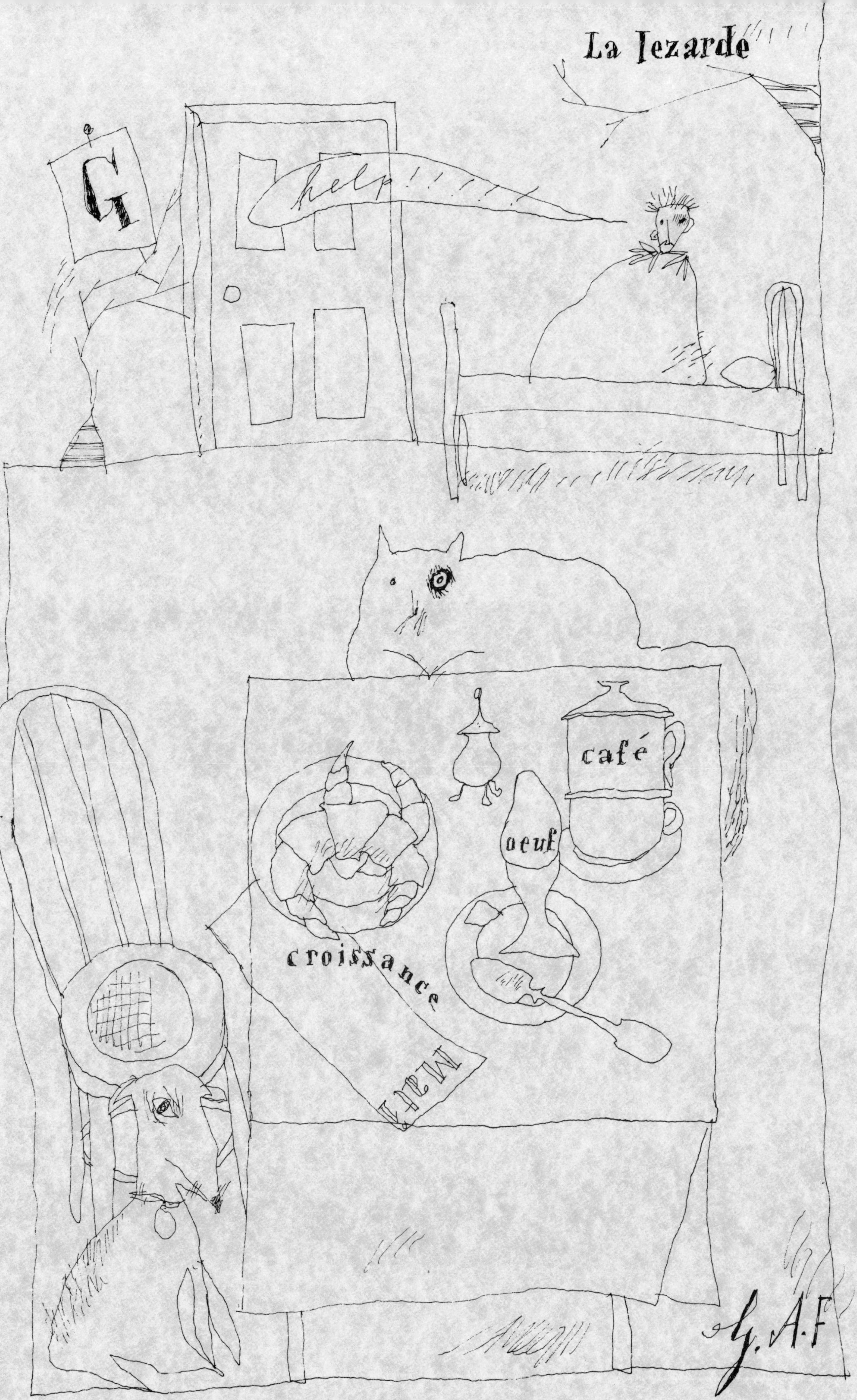
La Jezarde
G
help!!!!!
café
oeuf
croissance
Mail
G.A.F

unable to purchase scissors until I find the French for them. 'Scission' in French means scission in English, which I have never heard of, and it is not that because I asked for it yesterday in a shop and met with blank looks, shrugs and finally a string of sausages. How could Papa do this to me).

To continue with the Method: Having marked a word, I then teach myself the English for it. I think, in time, this will greatly broaden my knowledge of the language. I then use these words, wherever possible to illuminate my sketches.

This way I have already learned:

la soucoup...the saucer
le lezard ...the lizard
la lezarde...the crack

(my fingernail settled at a point precisely between the last two, so I committed them both to memory)

and ordure...filthy.

The streets here are extremely 'ordure'. Horses should always reside in the country. How is Bonny? How I long to be back at the Manor.

I do not understand the French at all. Yesterday my landlady came to collect my rental. I was still in my night attire, having been kept awake by yet another party downstairs. She insisted on grasping me and attempted to look under my nightshirt. I struggled, but in no time she had me on the listing bed. I could see my allowance vanishing again and I fought valiantly. However, she is a large, determined woman, reeking of garlic and I was no match for her.

Madame Leclerc.

I was in full expectation of her then relieving me of all my monies, but she left without even taking my rental. Unfortunately I feel sure she will return for it when she gets her breath (ordure) back. It would be agreeable if she forgets, but not very French.

The whole bed smells of garlic.

Do prevail on Papa to rescue me from this barbarous country and dispatch the Dictionary with all expedition.

Your loving brother,

Godwyn

G.A.F. 1900

G. Ainsley Ffrench.

Montmarte,
April.

My dear sister,

April in Paris is hateful. The weather is changeable and everyone has influenza, in consequence of which they all now breathe through their mouths, and venturing forth is truly an ordeal.

This attic is freezing, the windows are full of lezards (see my last letter, Augustine), and I am fast approaching the last of the canvasses and tapers. They may see me through the summer, but what of next winter, if I am to continue my incarceration here? You must persuade Papa to allow me to return to the Manor, or I will surely catch my death.

Madame Leclerc did not return for my money last month. This I took to be some recompense for the garlic on the sheets, so I have smiled at her a good deal, which, on reflection, I do not think such a clever idea as she is then inclined to hug me. One of these days the fumes may cause me to vomit on her bosom, which already seems to have foodstuffs dangling from it. Perhaps she has hugged someone else before me.

I have no doubt that garlic must be a major hazard for those who undertake the Grand Tour. Unfortunately, sister, this would be comp-

Rupalley Cycles ALUMINIUM
BUVEZ
À LA BONNE SOURCE
ROTATIVE AUTOMATIQUE ECONOMIE de TEMPS et de TRAVAIL
ROUE
Absinthe
HÔTEL
CLEMENT
Gᴰᴱ PHARMACIE
COMMERCIA
BIERE
BOULANGERIE PATISSERIE Sᵀ MEDARD
COSSER
Cabaret
FOLIES
LES FOLIES BERGERES
MOUTARD
Meres
MUSIC-HALL
Cafe des ARTISTES
CAFE
GROS
ROI des CAFÉS
CHOCOLAT
VINAY
PETITE MAISON
TABLEAUX VIVANTS
BAR
VINS
CORBEILLES et MARIAGES
HORLOGERIE ORFÉVRES
VINS
VIN
G. Ainsley Ffrench.

letely beyond your understanding, as you have never travelled anywhere.

With the money I was able to save on the rental, I had the sheets washed at the laundry (there are some very forward ladies there), I bought a pocket watch (the time does seem to be the same as ours) and a pair of gloves.

I cannot help but think that should the same thing occur again with the paying of the rental, it is well worth the cost of washing as the other financial benefits are so encouraging.

This morning Madame Leclerc caught me on the stair and licked my ear.

Thankfully, the African lady seems to be laid low in bed for most of the

time. I think she may have the influenza and a very small room. Her many gentlemen friends crowd the stairs as they await admittance and continually hamper my progress. They may, of course, be her doctors, or possibly, by now, mortitians. How would I know, when I cannot find the words?

I have just fed another canvas to the fire. In all honesty, apart from the aroma, I believe I am doing the world a service. You would not believe how bad they are.

I have now learned:

seance.... to sit

toise.... fathom

and moustache. moustache.

Madame Leclerc has a 'moustache'.

And an ordure bosom.

From your loving brother,

Godwyn.

P.S. The Dictionary has not yet arrived, Augustine.

Yr brother,

G.

Montmartrer,
May.

Dearest Augustine,

The worst has happened.

There I was this morning, in my nightshirt, waiting for Madame Leclerc to come and forget the rental again, when in rushed her husband, Monsieur Leclerc.[1] He shook his fist at me and shouted loud French questions and, despite my studies, I could not understand a single word he said.

I attempted a smile, which certainly seems to work with Madame, and that is when it happened. He hit me. I was quite unprepared. It was a most dastardly attack and he is an ordure brute.

My spectacles were knocked to the floor and after that, I was, of course, at his mercy. He punched me on the nose, seized my money and left, all the while bellowing at me in French. I have never been so miserable in my life. To think Papa would let me come to this.

My nose is still bleeding and I have just smudged my latest watercolour with it. I do not even know the French for blood. Perhaps it is 'blood'. I will look it up.

Now there is blood all over the dictionary as well.

7 Place Pigalle
AU CHIEN MORT
MENU
Place Pigalle
Place Pigalle
Vins
7
Viandes
CAFÉ
Sardines Saucisson Harengs marines
Oeufs au beurre noir
Goujons frits
Saucisses plates aux Choux
Terrine de Bordeaux
Cervelle beurre noir
Viande froide rémolade
Haricots flageolets
Salade
Poires Raisin Noir
Poissons
Bières
Monsieur Leclerc
by
G. Ainsley Ffrench.
Service Non Compris

I have learned:

blottin.... to crouch
and blouse .... blouse

but not blood. You can see the urgency with which I require the English-French dictionary, sister.

If I had blottired he might have missed me.

I can see the necessity to extend my studies. Because of my lack of French I am unable to determine the cause of the onslaught. Was it the incest or the rental, do you think? Judging from my previous experiences, [illegible] I would say that in England it would be the incest and in France the money. But how am I to acertain this? My mind is in turmoil.

And now there are two handkerchiefs to be washed. I am almost too upset to continue. Paying the rental has come as a great blow to me.

Please tell Papa (not of the incest as it seems to annoy him) of my straightened circumstances and beg him to relent.

I await the arrival of my Dictionary with much anticipation, Augustine.

Excuse the blood,

Your bleeding brother,

Godwyn

P.S. I have just had a visitation from the African lady. She saw my distress and gave me coffee and 'croissance' (which the dictionary says is 'growth', but actually is something you eat. Perhaps they grow it here). She then took off my nightshirt. I thought to wash it, but it was not to be. (So now there are two handkerchiefs, one nightshirt and the sheets again for the laundry).

G.

P.P.S. The African lady appears to be quite well, though it is difficult to tell from her colour, she has obviously recovered from her indisposition. I do not think she has a husband, at least I hope not. She has a remarkably clean bosom, considering where she comes from.

Yr bro,

G.

Montmatre,
June.

My dearest sister,

You will be pleased to hear that my fortune has, of a sudden, changed. My nose is returning to it's normal shape, the black eyes have faded and shrunk and I am in much better heart.

It all happened thus: Last week I chanced to be at the 'Gare Du Nord' (in English, the railway station). I go there on occasion to hear English spoken as I become dreadfully tired of French. It is quite like being at home when the five o'clock train comes in and everyone shouts.

There are never enough 'porters' (French for porters), so I offered my help to a large English gentleman with fine 'moustaches' and a beard. I carried his cricket bag for him. His luggage was marked 'Dr Grace'[1] and that of his friend 'Dr Watson', I noticed.

After I had shewn them to their barouche (I am as yet unacquainted with the French for barouche), they spoke very civilly to me. I told them I was here to study French and painting, which is the truth as that is what I am doing. They then handed me a large gratuity before being driven away. This struck me as a quite excellent way to supplement my

paltry allowance. For not only was I performing a useful service, I was also employing my knowledge of the English language, (I have worried that my lack of spoken English could lead to it's decline).

Without delay I hurried back to the train and was in good time to assist two more couples with their baggage, with the same pleasing results.

Soon I shall have enough froncs to leave Montmatre. I shall travel, I think. I may go to Africa.

My new French words are:

cout... cost
echelle.. ladder
le pigeon.. the pigeon
la tete.. the head

I take my dictionary with me to the railway station, in case the trains are late, and, as you can see, my vocabulary grows by the day. Soon I may put it to use.

I will enclose a sketch I made of my first two customers, the Doctors. The only paper I had with me at the time was some P. Ruiz had scribbled on. You will find my drawing in the centre of the page, where he had left a small space. You may well be beset by nightmares should you look at his

HÔTEL de la LOUCHE
27, RUE de la CATASTROPHE,
PARIS
Precious little room for my own work on what remains of the paper. G.A.F.
Café-Restaurant de la Place Blanche
DEJEUNERS, DINERS, SOUPERS
ÉTABLISSEMENT OUVERT TOUTE LA NUIT
La Moustache
Le Pigeon
La tête
La Blouse
Paris
J.D.W
A quick sketch of my first two customers at the Gare du NORD G.A.F.
TOTAL
ZE

likenesses, but bear in mind Augustine, these are the very people that Papa has forced me to live and sleep with in Monmartre.

Madame Leclerc never forgets the rental anymore. Her black eye is now yellow, though she seems unable to open it. I wish that he had hit her on the mouth. She has an echelle in her stocking.

The African lady has returned twice and not yet taken any of my money. She has a pet goat in her room.

I think I am fast becoming a citizen of the world. Travel is indeed broadening.

Your loving brother,

Godwyn

P.S. I will still have need of the dictionary for my studies, sister.

Yr lo. bro.

G

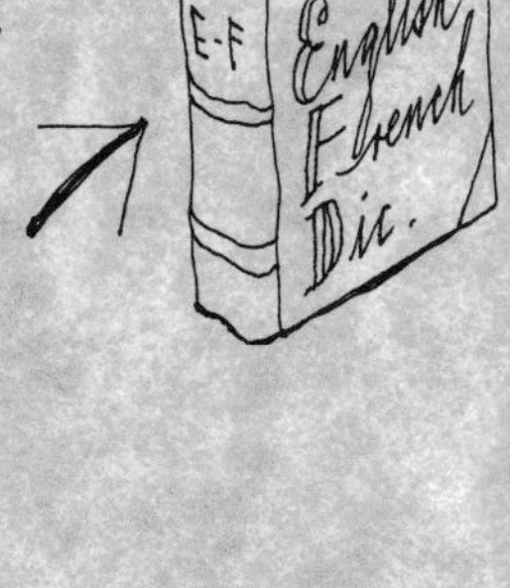

L'Ordure
La Moustache
L'Abandon
VIN
ROUGE
G. Ainsley Ffrench.

Montmarte,
July.

My dear Augustine,

It has been more than a month since my last letter. The most terrible disaster overtook me and I could not bring myself to write of it to you. Even now, I find myself unable to recount it without trembling.

You will recall that I wrote you of my services to the English at the Gare du Nord (the railway station). Well, dear sister, it is all over. Finished. I have never been so 'abaissement' in my life.

For weeks I went each day to the railway station. All of my employers were most courteous and generous when they found that I was English, and I had great expectations that soon I would be leaving this horrid attic. However, my hopes were dashed on that last afternoon at the station, when I was savagely set upon by uncivilized French 'porters'.

They assaulted me, knocked me to the ground, dragged me to an alley, where they proceeded to remove my trousers. They then left me, in great disarray in the gutter (very ordure). Unfortunately they were still in possession of my trousers, with the whole week's gratuities in the pocket.

My ear was swelling alarmingly and once more my nose was bleeding, this time all over my shirt. Sister, I have told you of my troubles with the laundresses, now, without trousers, what hope would I have?

Just then a large person (I thought it a horse, at first) landed on top of me and all the breath was quite knocked out of me. The person supposed that he had been the cause of my nose bleed and offered me his handkerchief with many apologies.

Noting my lack of trousers, he introduced himself as Osher Wile.[1] A strange name, but nonetheless a gentleman, and English. You can well imagine my relief. It transpired that he had suffered similar indignities to mine, from the waiters in the station diningroom. His speech was rather slurred, but this he said was due to the weather. There followed a long and vigourous discussion about the behaviour of the French in general. To tell the truth, he did most of the talking as he is a prodigious talker, and I was still trying to staunch the nose bleed.

He is a most charming man, slightly eccentric, I fancy. He

HÔTEL
HOTEL
ANGELUS
LIQUEUR
BEC
BAUER
MOET
et
CHANDON
VINS
PRESSEZ
Tous les soirs
BRUANT
au
MIRLITON
BOCK
13 Sous
ZAN
ELIXIR
Mr. Osher Wile.
G. Ainsley Ffrench.

wears a small lettuce in his buttonhole. In no time I found I had told him the whole story of the incest. He was not the least taken aback, in fact it seemed to amuse him a good deal and he insisted that I immediately accompany him to his hotel. I have the address written, even now, on my shirt cuff, (in actual fact, his shirt cuff, as he was kind enough to give me a change of clothes). The hotel is called the Hotel D'Alsace, where I was somewhat puzzled to find that the staff refer to him as Mosieur Malmoth.[2] I suspect that 'Osher Wile' could well be a pseudonym.

In fact, I fear he may be what Pater refers to as 'a bounder'. He told me a story, which he professes is the truth, a story so obviously fabricated, that I will not bore you with it, my dear Augustine. Suffice it to say, that it ended with him being exiled from England for something called boggery, which he explained was more to his taste than incest. He then offered to show me the boggery after dinner.

Alas, it was then I discovered that my new friend is incapable of telling the truth, as it

turned out to be nothing more than that which Mister Wiggins[3] our tutor, and I did every Thursday at the Manor.

I am, fortunately, wise enough in the ways of the world to know that one cannot entirely trust the word of a man who wears a vegetable on his lapel.

However, he is such excellent company that I will not hold his pretensions against him. We are to meet again the day after tomorrow.

We speak in English most of the time, but he has been of great help with my French. From him I learned:

grand.... big
bow .... beautiful
onnuyer.... bore.

From my dictionary;
pie... a magpie
louche... a soup ladle
clou... a nail.

As you can see, I am not wasting my time here. By the way, I used dear Osher's scissors to cut my 'clous'.

Have you broached the subject of the increase in my allowance with Papa yet? I feel I may well be

rather short this week, as I need extra froncs for the laundry. I must have Osher's clothes washed so I can return them to him.

I hope the English-French Dictionary has not gone astray in the mail, sister, as I am not yet in receipt of it,

Your brother,

Godwyn

Motmartre,
August.

Dear Augustine,

Your last note to me made no mention at all of an increase in my allowance, or of the French-English Dictionary. I am shocked. I cannot believe that members of my family would leave me in this truly desperate position in Paris, now my work at the railway has ceased.

As it happens, I have another request, which I trust will not be equally ignored.

Please, dearest sister, could you look out my last letter to see if I mentioned Mister Osher Wile's address? I have a mind I did, and I have need of it with the utmost urgency.

I was to have dinner and boggery with him some time ago. However, I took the shirt, with his address written on the cuff, to the laundry and they have scrubbed it clean. I have searched and searched and cannot find his hotel again.

He had offered to accompany me to a grand Exposition that is on in Paris at the moment, which he says is all run by the new electrisity. Though I know full well that he is an astonishing liar on occasion, I would very much like to see him again. He does seem to have excellent French

and he could be of great help with my vocabulary.

Please, Augustine, I beg you to put his address on a post card post haste.

I met the two English doctors, my first customers on the railway, in the Bois de Boulogne (timber from Boulogne) the other day, as I was looking for Osher's hotel, and they confirmed that there really is an exposition, so I am pleased to be able to report that my new friend does not always practice perversion.

The doctors were attempting to teach some Frenchmen how to play cricket. They introduced me to a friend of theirs, a French midget called 'Teapot'[1], who, they said, drew too. Doctor Grace said that he is a Comt, which is a Count in French, but I think that he was only joshing. Perhaps the Count is like Tom Thumb in the circus (see Modern Marvels) who was referred to as 'The General'. In any event, the Count knows my African lady, and I already knew the Count. I had made a sketch of him a few months ago as he waited on the landing outside her room. Is it not a small world, sister?

MESSAGERIES MARITIMES
LE PAQUEBOT NEWHAVEN-DIEPPE

G. Ainsley Ffrench.

The Count borrowed my paintbox and made a sketch of me. It was quite dreadful, but I did not say so, as he has enough troubles, I should think, being a midget.

I had made a sketch of the 'Bois' for you, but the Count ruined it by adding, amid much jocularity, several naked, dancing ladies, who were not there at all. I did not remonstrate with him, because of his affliction, but put the offensive page away and started on another. There was a duel taking place at the time, (indeed, it is difficult to find a time when one is not), and keeping my paints firmly by my side, I made a drawing of it and sought the Count's assistance only with the French language. In this manner I learned:

la lune.... the sun
le mouchoir.... a fly
un gentilhomme
anglaise.... a Bulgar
lui-meme..., Louis the Fifth
and matin.... a duel.

You can now see how writing words on my paintings helps my French studies. However, I still have great need of the English-French Dictionary.

La Lune
Au Clair de la Lune
Monsieur Le Comte
de Perrier-sur-Mer
lui-même
Le
Mouchoir
Un
Gentilhomme
Anglais.
G. Ainsley-Ffrench.
Matin dans Le Bois de Boulogne

The African lady and Madame Leclerc continue their visits, which incline to be tedious as neither of them attempt to speak English with me. I cannot ask the African lady of her business with the Count (Teapot) as I do not have the words for it.

I am truly anxious to see my dear friend Osher again, so please, please hurry with his address.

You could enclose it with the dictionary,

Your expectant brother,

Godwyn.

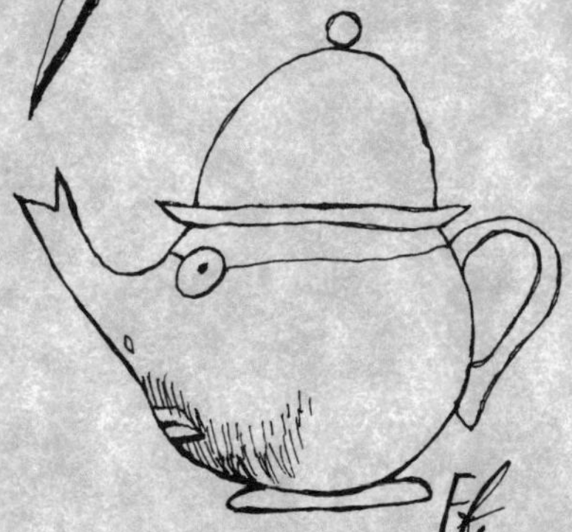

Why my friend
is called Teapot?
I don't know.

Montmatre,
September.

My dear Augustine,

I do not understand you at all. What is it that you are going on about? Your complaint that I wrote of nothing but dear Osher in my last letter is ridiculous. Why shouldn't I write of him? He showed me great kindness and generousity. Now I wish to thank him and return his clothes, and I need his address to so do.

I am afraid that you had cried into your letter, Augustine, and that made it very difficult to decipher. A clear hand was never one of your strong points in any case. Poor, dear Osher's address was completely obliterated. Perhaps when you have pulled yourself together, sister, I could have the address again, as it does happen to be of the utmost importance.

In my last letter I did not comment on the fact that you are with child, because I chose to ignore it. How you could write thus to me, when you are not yet married, I do not know. Surely you realize what that makes the child. I felt, under the circumstances, that not mentioning your plight was the most civilized thing to do. I would encourage you toward the same standard of behaviour.

I have made a momentous decision in my life. I am going to teach English. Even now I am printing a poster to that effect to hang in the bar next door. I have given it much thought and feel I am well equipped for it, as my English is far better than any spoken here, except, naturally, for the English. The Dictionary is now crucial, Augustine.

I have no money at all, and even if I had, I doubt I would dare go again to the laundry, since the last time I was there the scrubbers surrounded me and attacked.

I felt very much as Colonel Custer must have at his last stand. (see Modern Marvels on the Natives of America). And so my sheets are becoming very ordure. The African lady does not appear to notice, which is not surprising, as I do not think they have sheets in the jungle; nor does Madame Leclerc, which is also not surprising, considering the state of her.

Think on my sufferings, Augustine, rather than your own. You remain at the Manor and are clothed and fed. I do not know why you should need an allowance, even if you are carrying a bastard. And do try not to cry over

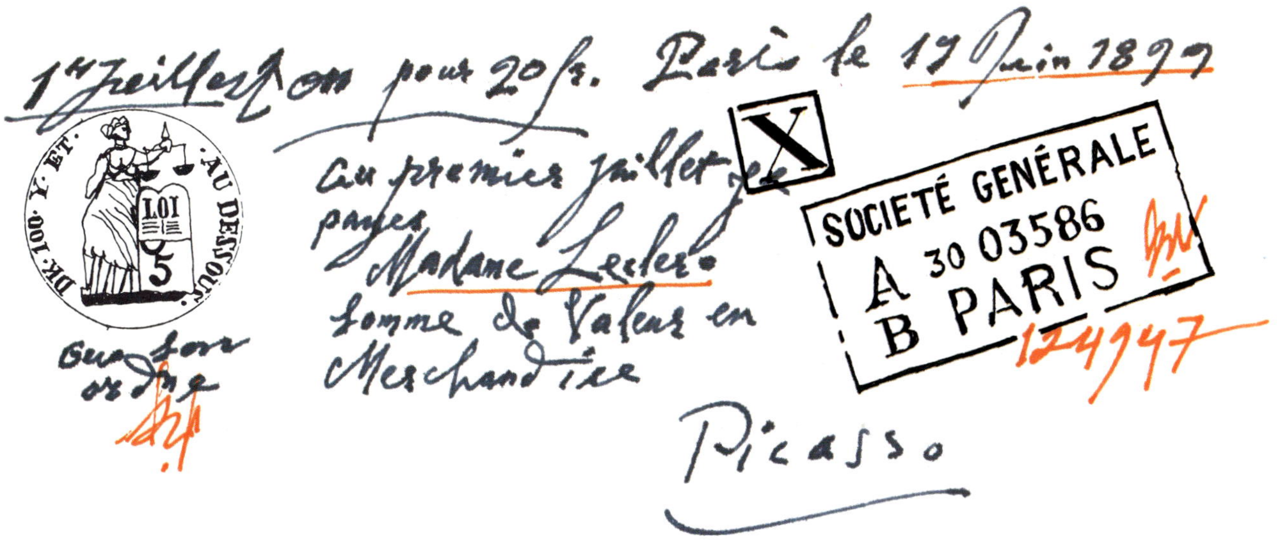
Paris le 17 Juin 1897
DK·100·Y·ET·AU DESSOUS
LOI
5
Au premier juillet je payer Madame Leclerc Somme de Valeur en Merchandise
X
SOCIETÉ GENÉRALE
A 30 03586
B PARIS
124747
Picasso

G. Ainsley Ffrench.
21
Le Bollard
La Laundrette

your letters. It quite ruins the receiving of them if one cannot read them.

My new French words are:

paperasse.... old paper
mole.... mole
and fenetre.... window.

All Madame Leclerc says to me is 'veet' which I am sure she thinks is my name, though I have now corrected her a hundred times. All my African lady ever says is 'merd' which is not in the dictionary either, so I fancy it is African. So much for their help with my studies.

Now, Augustine, you really must take a grip of yourself, send me the dictionary and the address and if you are truly with child, get married before you disgrace us all.

Write soon and try not to cry on it,

Your brother,

Godwyn

or La
Le Bastard.

Mandelthorpe Manor,
Wednesday
25th
02

My dear God

I

how could you

child

I

canne
never
I Papa

love

just

P.S. Hotel

Montmatre,
October.

Dear Augustine,

You have done it again. Your last letter arrived here sodden. How could you have so little thought for me.

You have now been crying, by my count, for almost a month.

Your letter reads thus; Dear God--- (splodges) ---- I ---- how could you-------------------child-----------------I-----cannot-----ever----so---I
---I----Papa---------love------gust
P.S. Hotel-----------

I stare at it and hold it to the light, but can make no sense of it. I do not know how to reply except to say that I hope you are better and soon cease this astonishing deluge.

I am afraid I am still awaiting news of Osher's address. A small piece of paper with the name of the hotel would be sufficient. Try holding the paper at arm's length as you write.

My news will certainly cheer you. My circumstances are improving at last.

The advertisement I placed in the bar next door, offering my services in English, has had surprising results. I now have five paying customers who come regularly and several others who are less commit-

ted. I speak to them throughout in nothing but English, which. I admit, is bad for my French, but good for their vocabularies. I know Mister Wiggins[1] would be proud of me. His time at the Manor was certainly not wasted.

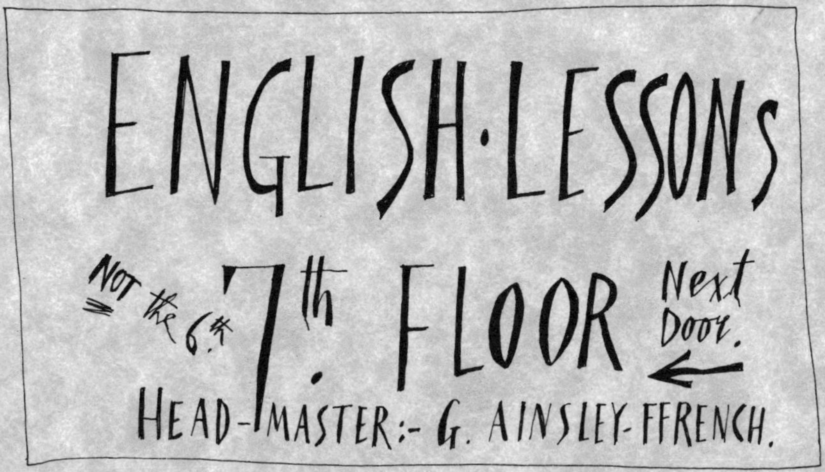

One of my students, a young Frenchman called Umberto Zombini,[2] presented me with a ticket to the circus last week. To my astonishment, I found that he and his whole family were performing there. I am sending one of the posters of their act, as they were just before the accident. In my excitement, I had waved at Umberto and called out his name. He never should have waved back, I fear, he was on the bottom, and the wave brought the whole 'Humane' (French for humane) 'Pyramide'[3] (French for pyramid) crashing to the ground.

Les ZOMBINIS
SORTIE
Chaque Soir à 8h.
12
13
14
GRANDE · CIRQUE · GOUNOD.

Fortunately, Umberto was not one of those taken to the hospital, and I know you will be pleased to hear that our lessons have, in no way, been affected.

There was a lady on the programme who bore a remarkable resemblance to my African lady. Her name was Fifi La Blanche.[4] She wears high boots and very little else and cracks a long whip at some horses. The horses did not seem to do very much, but the audience became wildly excited. I waved and shouted to her as well, but by then everyone was waving and shouting, so I do not know if it was her or not.

On my African lady's next visit, I attempted to ask her about the circus, using sign language. I do not know quite what happened, but afterwards I was not able to sit down for a week. Now, when she comes up the stairs (I can always tell, from the cracking of the whip), I have taken to hiding myself under the bed (she never looks. She just says 'merd' and leaves. Madame Leclerc always looks and then says 'veet').

You can see from the above, Augustine, that my need for the dictionary is dire.

To inspire you, I will send you the drawing I did some time ago of poor little 'Teapot'. It will make you feel much better to think of yourself as a midget.

Of course I know you are very small, but you are not a real midget.

I am, when time allows, continuing my studies. Here are my new words:

frottir... to rub
meugler... to moo
and clavicule... collarbone.

I passed Madame Leclerc on the stairway to-day, and she frottined me while she hugged me.

Do stop crying, Augustine, and send me the Dictionary, and Osher's address (again), and should Papa be considering sending me extra monies, pray do not mention my good fortune with the School of English.

Your brother,

Godwyn
(Headmaster.)

P.S. You may tell Nanny[5] and Mister Wiggins.
Yr lov. brot.
G. (H.M.)

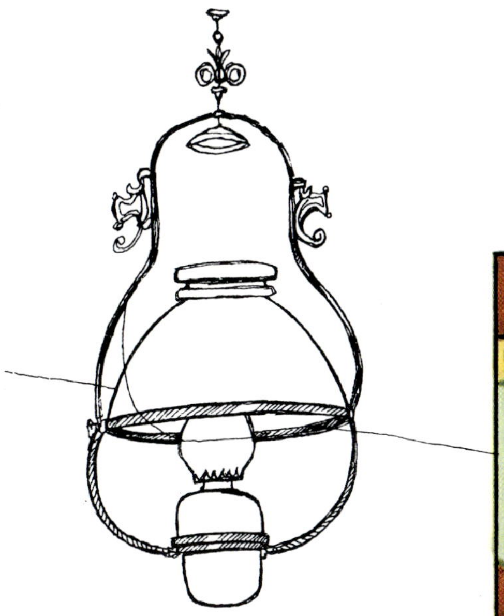

G. Ainsley Ffrench.

Montmarter,
November.

Dear Augustine,

Thank you for your letter, and thank you for the brave attempt you made to keep the pages dry, even though it was not entirely successful.

It was a great pity that, once more, the lower half of the paper was reduced to a swampy mess, as I feel sure that that is where you had written Osher's address.

I know I had forgotten that you were shortsighted when I suggested you wrote your letters holding the paper at arm's length, but, bear in mind Augustine, you do have exceedingly short arms.

Have you thought of using a handkerchief? If the conventional manner of using one fails, why not tie it around your nose, as the outlaws and bush-rangers do? This way, you would contain not only the tears, but also the effluvium from your nasal passages. Or perhaps a mask might better serve the purpose. I recall seeing an excellent clown's mask in the nursery.

Sister, at the risk of causing yet another torrent of tears, I must tell you that I am more than a little out of patience with you. I truly do not understand how you could lose a baby.

You do not go out of the house that often, and surely, if you lost it indoors, one of the staff would help you look for it. Ask Nanny,[1] for she is remarkably good at finding things. Remember my velocipede?

Or, then again, you could always look on the bright side. Has not the cheering thought occurred to you that, for the sake of the family name, it may be a blessing that the little ~~bast~~ baby has wandered off?

Your letter could not have come at a worse time for me, as I was already deeply troubled by my own situation.

The police have raided my School and forced me to close it. They have confiscated all my fees, and I am now desolate and destitute.

To tell the truth, I have never been so miserable in all my life.

Perhaps, if I had been in possession of the Dictionary, I may have been able to avert the course of justice. As it happened, however, I did not have the necessary words.

I think, sister, that this is not the time to dwell on thoughts of yourself and your carelessness, but rather to reflect on the tragedy which has befallen me. Why you have sent me not one penny from your

HÔTEL POE
103, Rue Morgue, Paris.
le balon.
Umberto, Friend & Pupil
le garçon.
G.A.F.
Montmatre 1900

allowance, I am unable to understand. This would seem to be an opportune time for you to make amends. I shall starve without the froncs from the school, I know I shall.

It is also because of your queer behaviour that I am unable to find dear Osher, and am therefore friendless. Umberto fled from his family on their return from the hospital, and I could not quite grasp where he was going. Teapot has gone to the country. He sent me a drawing which I will send on to you, as I do not care for it very much.

Further to that, a post card has arrived from P. Ruiz Picasso. I fear that he may be returning at any moment to take over my attic, or possibly not, as his writing confounds me. I shall enclose it with this letter, as I do not want Madame to see it. I would be grateful if you could find someone to decipher it and send me the meaning.

So now, as you can read, I am possibly homeless and alone. Apart from Madame Leclerc, whose absence is her best feature, and my African lady. My African lady has taken to bringing me gifts of Absinthe (a strong drink from Africa) and packets of white

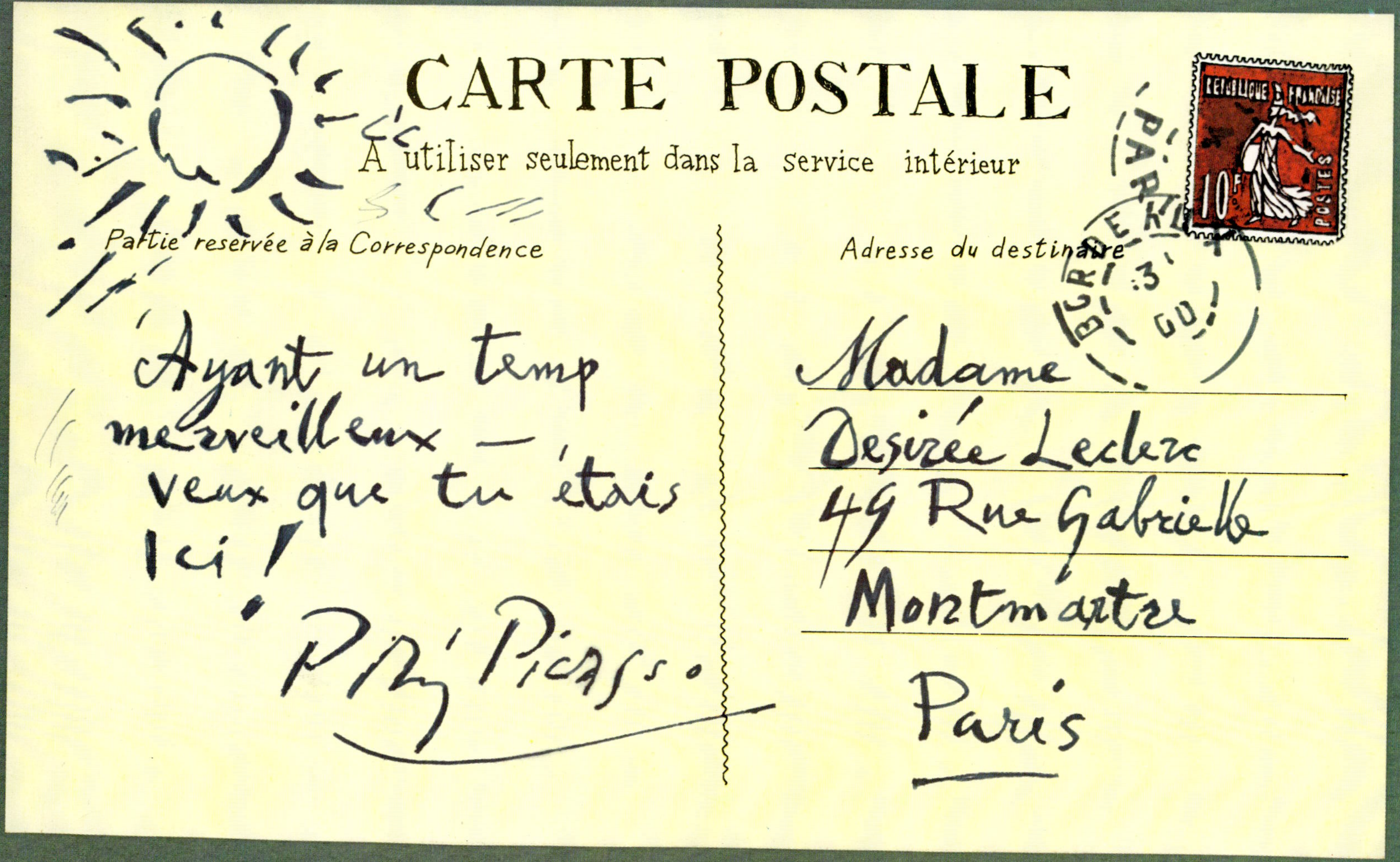
CARTE POSTALE

A utiliser seulement dans la service intérieur

Partie reservée à la Correspondence

Ayant un temp
merveilleux —
veux que tu étais
ici!

P.R. Picasso

Adresse du destinaire

Madame
Desirée Leclerc
49 Rue Gabrielle
Montmartre
Paris

powder (they do not seem to have it in tins as we do in England). I drank the Absinthe, but it made me ill, and I put the powder in my shoes, to stop them chafing. It was most successful.

I have learned some new French words, but I fear my heart is not in it any more;

chien.... dog
serment.... oath
noel.... Christmas (which seems to be a very odd name for the Festive Season, as the only Noel I know is that grubby chap who lives in one of the workmen's cottages).

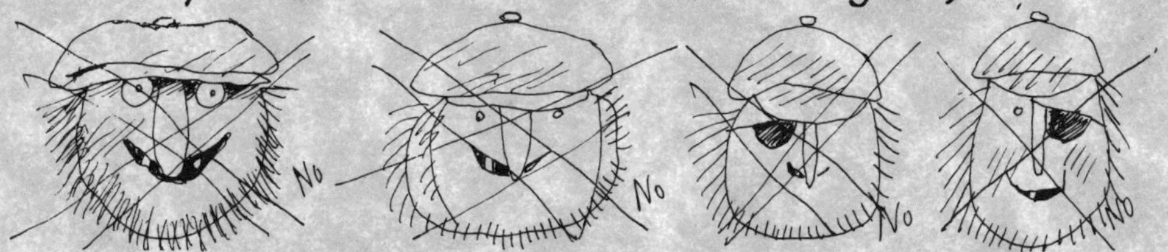

I shall post this letter to-day, I think. The Post Office is some distance away, and as my shoes still pinch, I will call in downstairs to see if my African lady has more powder for them. She may be a grotesque, but she is a nicer person than I thought, even if her gifts do make me sick.

Please, old thing, pull your wits together, find the child or not, post the Dictionary, send Osher's address and enclose some money (perhaps my Christmas present). If it is necessary, wrap your head in a towel.

I remain,
Your brother,

Godwyn.

P.S. I had already sealed this letter, but opened it to recount the following: I went to collect the powder for my shoes, making my way cautiously downstairs, as there are several goats now tethered on the landing. One of the goats butted me and precipitated me through my African lady's door. She was in the bed with Mosieur Leclerc. And Mosieur Leclerc is not Mosieur Leclerc at all. He is another Madame Leclerc. He is a lady. Or at least he has all the outward signs of one, and none of those of a gentleman.

To think that I was once punched by ~~him~~ her. I can only say how glad I am that I never attempted to hit ~~him~~ her back.

Nevertheless, two black eyes and a bloddy nose from a lady. I am shocked, sister. I feel I may not recover.

On top of which, the African lady did not seem to understand my request (in sign language) for the shoe powder. So now my feet will hurt all the way to the beastly Bureau de Poste (the Post Office, Augustine).

Yr bro.

G.

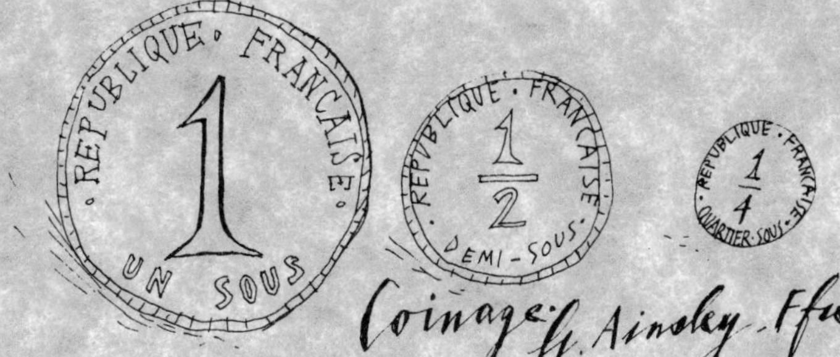

Coinage: G. Ainsley-Ffrench.

Montmarte,
December.

Dear Pater,

It is with the most heartfelt joy that I received your letter and the news that you are allowing me to return to the Manor.

Paris has indeed been a profound lesson to me. You have my solemn word that I will have no more incest with my sister, Augustine. In that respect I am truly reformed.

May I take this opportunity to offer my congratulations on your elevation to Leader of the House of Commons. I assure you that I am fully aware of the responsibility this now imposes on all of us.

Opening my ~~School~~ very successful School of English in Paris has, as you so rightly say, made a man of me. As for your suggestion that I may well have the family bent for politics, I can only reply that I now feel I am ready for anything, Sir.

I have missed you all frightfully, and look forward to being back at the Manor in time for Noel (that's Christmas in French, Sir), if my train fare is not delayed by the seasonal post.

I remain, as always,

Your respectful son,

Godwyn.

P.S. Please thank Augustine for sending me the French-English Dictionary for Christmas, even if it was not the one I wanted.

Your son,

Godwyn.

P.P.S. Please do not worry yourself any longer over the unfortunate accident to Bonny, Sir. I was glad to hear that your new horseless carriage sustained no serious injuries.

As before,

Godwyn.

MESSAGERIES MARITIMES

LE PAQUEBOT NEWHAVEN-DIEPPE

Oh Rivoir, Paris!

THE TIMES SATURDAY SEPTEMBER 3 1939

osé

, I hadn't
rly on by
shoes on
t of their
/or raised
g remarks
e a whole
t that they
so as to
to grow
carry on
oes with
n't seem
er.
, the
ind so
eing a
ar more
mbarrass-
n.
possible
ut bitter
k patent
icious. I
ed just
tired of,
me and
so as to
ther.
ys' shoes
simpler
ey're not
ted toe
hoes we
a good
d sense
either
equired
so we

taken
n, my
rancing
er pair
uff the
up the
ion but
alf the
yself.
stinctly
from
eassure
some
it was
by now

we had,
elimin-
size 6D
as the
king it
kely.
an who
he very
at they
we were

Galleries

THERE IS A MOST extraordinary retrospective exhibition on in Paris at the moment,which I urge you not to miss, 'Godwyn Ainsley Ffrench.in Paris, 1900'. At this time there would seem to be no intention of bringing this excellent exhibition to the attention of the British people, an omission I abhor.For this genius I am proud to say, is none other than an Englishman.

Write to your Member, petition your Council, harrass your local Gallery that you may view one of the Marvels of the Modern World.

I am not one to quibble, so I will come to the point at once-Ffrench's works are,in more ways than one, a revelation. And even though some mindless idiot from Paris has vandalized them all by scribbling over them (dare one point the paint brush?),they are, in my considerable opinion, masterpieces.

Ffrench's line and form bear a close resemblence to Picasso's, though these paintings and pictures from Ffrench's Paris period pre-date Picasso's accepted arrival in Paris by some months.

Ergo, let me place my neck on the guillotine and state that this exhibition proves, beyond all doubt, that Godwyn Ainsley Ffrench was the true genius and Picasso merely a slavish copyist.

SHAKE

This discovery of mine is bound to shake the Art World to its caw and have far reaching repercussions on the Dhow Jones Index.I go in fear of my life, an anomalous situation, I admit, for a fearless Art Critic. If you never hear of me again,it will be clear to you what has

Age

A small m
lation los
mud wa
lyte Ta
the D
Philosophy of
seventeenth cent
contained less th
people, a popul
that of Englan
that of France.
more pictures th
nation in the worl
one in every thre
paintings sold a
Dutch and most
seventeenth cent
den Age.
While the Itali
busy painting virg
scenes from cl
ology, Dutch pai
the course of ar
the ordinary wo
rounded them, f
with great relish.
landscapes with
classical nymph o
Egypt" to sugge
theme. They pain
rejoicing in the o
show off their skil
textures. They
scapes with
etched against
and fine skies.
And, most im
painted each ot
could serve as a
picture – a drunk
tavern, a love
daughter playin

CATALOGUE
of
A GRAND RETROGRESSIVE EXHIBITORY
by
Godwyn Ainsley Ffrench
"PARIS 1900."

TRANSMOGRIFIED FROM THE FRENCH BY
STEFAN STANISLAS POLAFSKY
PLOCK
POLAND

MRPZS.

Pomme du Jour,
144, Rue des Travesties,
Paris.

100f.

3rd September 1939.

The Pictures and Memorables of *Godwyn Aindey Ffrench* TRANSMOGRIFIED by S.S. POLAFSKY MRPZS

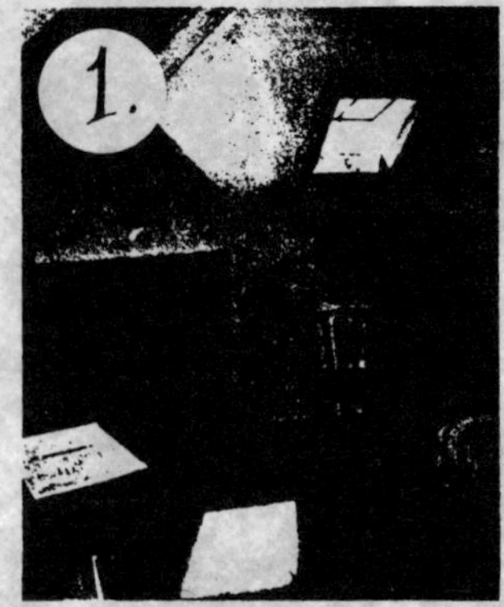

1. THE SPACE IN MONTMARTRE WHERE GODWYN SWINGS A CAT. *(PHOTOGRAVURE).*
2. A LAUNDER AT WORK. A SCRUBBER. *(COLOURED STICK ON CUSHION SHEATH).*
3. A CHAIR FIRED AND BROKENLY. *(PHOTOGRAVURE).*
4. MADAMD LECLERC IN ALL HER SKIN AND HAIR. *(FEMALE SWAN, FLUID AND RIVER HUES).*
5. STRANGERS WITH WIND IN A PARKING PLACE. *(SODDEN HUES AND SPLASHES).*

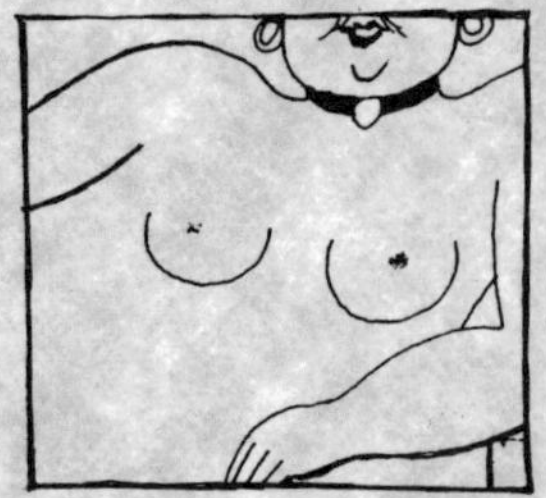

(4.) *A DETAILING.* (EXPLODED).

6. W.C. GRACE. THE HEROIN OF ENGLAND. *(SODDEN HUES AND WATER AND FEMALE SWAN).*
7. A CONGLOMERATE OF FLORALS IN A VESSEL SUBSISTING WITH DISTILLING APPARATUS. *(GREASE ON SOLICITED VOTES).*
8. A PICNIC ON THE HERBS. *(PHOTOGRAVURE).*
9. THE PLACE OF REST WHERE GODWYN WAS LAID EVERY NIGHTS. *(FEMALE SWAN ON A LARGELY PIECE OF SHEET).*

G. Aindey Ffrench. 1900.

10. GODWYN UPRIGHT WITHOUT THE BAR, AMBUSHED BY LOVED ONES DRINKED. *(PHOTOGRAVURE).*
11. FIFI LA BLANCHE TAMPERS WITH A POPULAR GOAT. *(GREASE ON SOLICITED VOTES).*

12. GODWYN REARING ON LA GOULIE, HIS EDGES IN VIEW. THE OTHERS WHO ARE YOU. *(PHOTOGRAVURE).*
13. UMBERTO ON THE PLACE OF REST. LAID BACK. *(PHOTOGRAVURE).*
14. GODWYN BY HIMSELF BY HIMSELF. *(GREASE ON BEHIND OF SOLICITOR'S VOTES).*
15. GREASE BEDABBLED FLOOR FROM THE GAROTTE IN MONTMARTRE. *(HONEST).*
16. UMBERTO WITH BUTTOCKS RESTING ON THE GROUND IN THE GLOOM OF A PERENNIAL PLANT. *(FAMALE SWAN AND FLUID).*

17. MISTER OSHER WILE IN THE BACKWARDS BRAIN OF GODWYN. *(FEMALE SWAN AND FLUID AND COLOURED STICKS).*

18. 'TEAPOT' UPRIGHT AND HANGING A PRETTY SILLY LITTLE WOMAN BY HAND (NOT VIEWING) FINGERING THE LOWER OF A LADY OF THE UNKNOWN. *(PHOTOGRAVURE).*

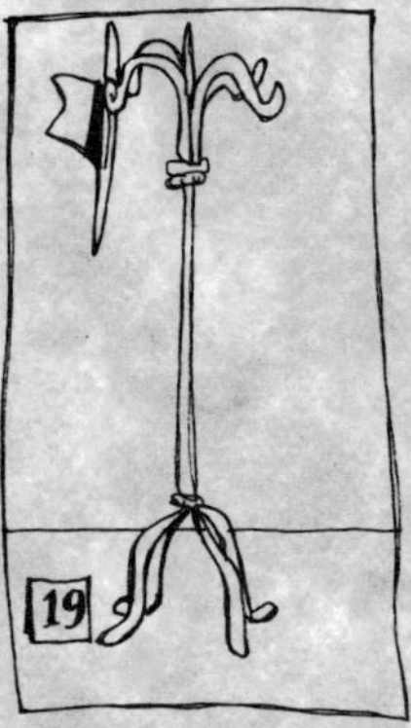

19. A HAT STANDING. *(HONEST).*

20. MADAME LECLERC BEING DECEITFUL ON THE PLACE OF REST WITH TWO SALMON ON HER LARGE STRONG BOX FOR SAILOR'S POSSESSIONS. *(FEMALE SWAN, FLUID AND COLOURED STICKS).*

21. A MERG FROM THE GAROTTE. *(HONEST).*

22. UMBERTO WITH TWO FOOT SHOWING. *(COLOURED STICKS ON SHEET).*

23. A CONCIERGE OF THE TYPE REBUILT FROM ONE HONEST STOCKING, ONE PROTECTIVE GARMENT AND ONE PAIR HONEST FOOLS OF THEMSELVES. PICKED UP BY ONE CAT. *(SQUASHED PAPER AND GREASE).*

24. A GOOD FOR NOTHING WOMAN WITH SOME LABELS. *(FEMALE SWAN AND FLUID).*

25. A PANORAMA OF PARIS MADE FAST TO SHOCK UMBERTO ON HER DAY OF BORNING. *(SPLASHES ON SHEET).*

26. THE AMOUNT OF ENTRY TO THE GAROTTE. *(HONEST).*

27. GODWYN WITH HIS BUTTOCKS RAISED ON A SEAT VERY ADJACENT TO THE APPARATUS FOR CREMATE VICTUALS. *(FEMALE SWAN, FLUID AND SODDEN HUES).*

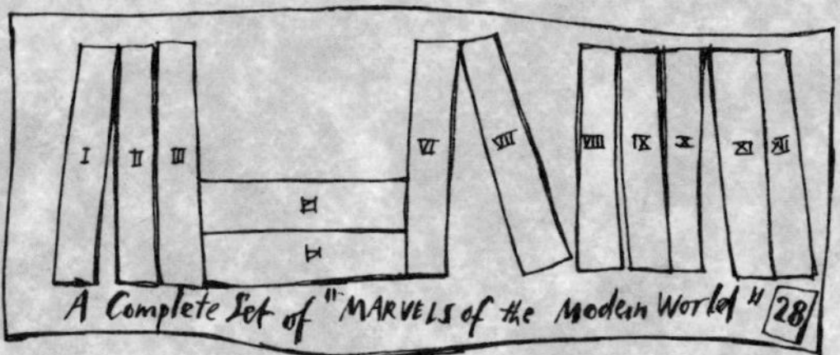

28. ONZE LEVRES EXCAVITE DE MAIDELTORP MAISON. LA SOURCE DES SAVOIRS FAIRES DE GODWYN. *(HONEST).*

29. TWO ENGLISHMANS CLOSE ALONGSIDE LA GOULIE IN THE PARKING PLACE WITH SMOKE ISSUING. *(A WICK OF LEAD IN TIMBER ON BULLET PAPER).*

30. GODWYN SURPRISED IN CAMERA WITH THE SANE. *(PHOTOGRAVURE).*

31. A ROLL IN THE MORNING WITH COFFEE BECOMINGLY COLD. ACCOMPANIED BY ONE EMBRYO. *(FEMALE SWAN AND FLUID).*

32. GODWYN TEARING AS HE OTTERS HIS TERMINALS TO MONTMARTRE, PICKED UP BY SOLICITOR'S VOTES SQUASHED BY HIS UNDERARMS, WITH A GOOD FOR NOTHING WOMAN IN HAND WITH LABELS. *(SODDEN HUES WITH SPLASHES WHEN HE WAS EXECUTED ON THE PARCEL SHIP MARCHING TO THE FAR EDGE OF THE FRENCH CHANEL).*

33. THE PLACE OF NORMAL LIVES, WITH TWO BUTTER BEASTS SHOCKED BY THE BACK VIEW OF GODWYN CHEWING COD. *(SODDEN HUES ON GREAT WESTERN RAILWAY CONVENIENCE PAPER).*

WHAT IS OTTERING THE DETRACTORS OF GODWYN AINSLEY FFRENCH.

Godwyn Ainsley Ffrench, the unnourishing artist belonging to Montmartre commencing this centuple was one. Critics of England show him their posterior and join the army. I I come upon you with surprise the artist whose technicals were stolen by Picasso after. Which emotion moves round with a spoon in a merg! Eyes overeat richly! The alcohol leaps high from your trunk! I sit with paws out for your missing piece. Do not stop for a short. Get out.
(Hyppolyte Carcasonne. FIGARO).

I am really please with me to have the knowing of Ainsley Ffrench from a hole sunk in the ground, centuries before. We persons are then very shut. Drunking wine and smashing breads accompanied. I go backwards in my brain and bump into one uncivilized mans living in Bohemia, but honest however he falls on the ground. Ah! My lover Ainsley! How the damp testimonials rear!

W.P.J. SNELL.

STEFAN STANISLAS POLAFSKY: Borning Plock, Poland. Member Royal Polish Zoological Soc. Otters in manys tongue. Transubstantiates regular. All knowing in Poland. Transformation welcomed.

P R I N T E D I N B Y D G O S Z C Z P O L A N D.

APPENDIX

LETTER DATED JANUARY. 1900.

1. This is, of course, the infamous Madame Desiree Leclerc of Montmartre, New York and Rio, though G.A.F. seems unaware of it at the time of writing.

   ADDITIONAL MATERIAL SEE: *'Famous Trials of 1902' pp 71-113.*

LETTER DATED FEBRUARY. 1900.

1. *'Marvels Of The Modern World'* was a set of encyclopaedias very popular with English upper classes at the time.
   See: G.A.F's Retrospective Catalogue (1950). Exhibit 28
2. P. RUIZ PICASSO. It is conceivable that this is the same artist who later became well known as Pablo Picasso, though experts agree that this pre-dates his accepted arrival in Paris by some months. However, bearing in mind G.A.F's opinion of the artist's work, it seems unlikely that it is the same man. It could, of course, be Pablo Picasso's little known cousin, but so little is known of him that we cannot confirm this.
3. Surely G.A.F. is here referring to Enrico Caruso, who is best remembered perhaps for not behaving very well during the San Francisco earthquake 1906.

LETTER DATED MAY. 1900.

1. V. J. LECLERC. Notorious associate of Desiree Leclerc. Chief suspect in the Case of the Leg in the Louvre, 1901, the Minced Chinaman at Maxims, 1901, the Voodoo Reign of Terror, 1902, and the strange affair of the Hand Sandwich, 1903. Finally brought to trial for the Rue de la Paix Garrottings in 1903, which were said to be acts of vengence against the deportation of Desiree Leclerc, 1902. Convicted of all 23 garrottings. Deported to Devil's Island 1903. Escaped 1903.

   SEE: *'Famous Trials of 1901'. 'Famous Trials of 1902', also 'Famous Trials of 1903'.*

   ADDITIONAL MATERIAL: *'Devil's Island Diary'*—V.J. Leclerc. *'I ate my way to Freedom'*—V. J. Leclerc. *'Rio Rita: The Truth'*—Juan Juandus. *'The Mad Beast of Manhattan'*—Shirley Cockran *'L 'Enemie Publique Nombre Un'*—Anon. *'Jacques: The Ripper?'*—Cordelia Winterbottom. *'I Left Her Heart In San Francisco'*—V. J. Leclerc.

LETTER DATED JUNE. 1900.

1. See: *'W. G. Grace's Last Case'*—W. G. Rushton, which proves the two gentlemen were in Paris at the time, if the book is to be believed.

LETTER DATED JULY. 1900.

1. There is no record of an Osher Wile in Paris at this time.

2. A Monsieur Sebastian Malmoth was registered at The Hotel D'Alsace during this period. G.A.F. could well be right in his assumption that 'Wile' was an alias.

3. WIGGINS. See: October Letter.

LETTER DATED AUGUST. 1900.

1. It is interesting to note that another midget painter in Paris at that time was the celebrated Toulouse Lautrec, whose nickname, curiously enough was 'Coffeepot'.

LETTER DATED OCTOBER. 1900.

1. Cecil Paradise Wiggins alias The Phantom Bantam, Dirty Dora and W. P. J. Snell. Left Maidelthorpe Manor in 1900 (while Godwin was abroad) after a particularly unsavoury incident. Moved to London where his new found affluence was rumoured by many to be directly related to blackmail activities. Secured a position as tutor at Buckingham Palace May, 1901. June, 1901 left suddenly for Australia. Scandal pursued him and after a brief stay he was deported to England. Jumped ship in Rio where he was reported to have masterminded 'The Grey Train Robbery' of 1902. In the ensuing chaos he fled to French Guiana and with the proceeds of the robbery acquired the largest cocaine plantation in South America, located 26 miles from the capital city of Cayenne. Within months he was known to the populace as Senor Grande. Driven from Guiana by the revolting peasants, he and his entourage (Les Anthropopagiques) commandeered the S.S. Rosalie, a rusting British hulk lying idle in the harbour, filled the hold with their cocaine harvest and sailed for New York. There they set up in business, under the patronage of one Leo The Ponce, selling 'Coca Cayenne Elixir of Life'. The rest is history.

   SEE: *'Buckingham Palace: A Personal Memoir'*—C. P. Wiggins. *'The Grey Train Robbery*—Juan Juandus. *'The Rape Of The Rosalie'*—Bernard Cripps. *'An Early History of the Emergence Of The Mobster In New York City'*—Alexander Pfeiffer. *'The Ponce and me: Just Good Friends'*—W. P. J. Snell.

2. UMBERTO ZOMBINI. Umberto Zombini, alias Alfredo Zorsa, Maxwell Bernini, Angelo Smith. Also known as 'The wop of Wapping' (London) and 'Angelface' (U.S.A.). Umberto, the seventh son in the Italian family Zombini, of circus fame, left Paris about this time and can then be traced to London, England, a move which may have been prompted by his lessons with G.A.F. His beginnings in London were humble. He ran an ice cream cart in Parliament Square, where he was fortunate enough to come under the protection of the then Leader of the House of Commons. This was of great assistance to him when he was accused, but subsequently acquitted, of the so-called 'Plague of Black Deaths' which resulted in the annihilation of many members of the Italian community. In 1901 he opened the prestigious gaming house "Il Casino di Pimlico'. His enemies maintained that he was an espionage agent, which would seem to be a gross libel as he remained on such excellent terms with so many members of His Majesty's Government. His casino was even said by some wits to have 'The Royal Seal of Approval'. He remained friendly with the Royal family even after his disgrace in 1903. Moved to New York, 1903. He was never in complete command of the English language and some felt that this could have contributed to the move. After changing his name in 1913 he became a household word in America.

SEE: *'Let Those Who are Without Sin'*—Hugo McVittie. *'Famous Trials of 1903'*, *'Great Courtroom Blockbusters 1905-1906'*. *'The Zorsa Case'*—Gideon Blade. *'Making Gelato The Easy Way'*—Maxwell Bernini. *'The Zombie Trial'*—Sheridan Harty. *'The Early History of the Emergence of the Mobster in New York City'*—Alexander Pfieffer. *'Prohibition: A National Disaster'*,—George Truman. *'Bernini Brewery. An American Dream'*—Jack Goodchild.

3. LA GRANDE PYRAMIDE HUMAINE. The name of the circus act of the Italian family Zombini. The act broke up about this time.

4. FIFI LA BLANCHE. Also known as Fifi Riffifi, La Goulie and Ffifi Ffrench. G.A.F. was correct. Fife La Blanche was employed by the Cirque during the latter months of 1900. She then left under a cloud of suspicion after the ritual murder of some performing goats. The modus operandi of this crime is noteworthy because it was exactly the same as that used later in the 'Voodoo Reign of Terror' (1902) and led to her immediate arrest.

   'Ah! Fifi La Blanche . . . a shiver of delight ran through me'. Andre Guillimot, Cirque Monde Gazette. 15.10.1900. *'Fifi La Blanche . . . with her boots and her whips. The audience held themselves, not breathing'*. Figaro. 9.9.1900. Fifi, a mulatto from French Guiana, was resident in Montmartre 1899-1903. Said

to be an exponent of the Black Arts, a drug smuggler and a murderess, she ostensibly earned a living through her expertise with whips. The citizens of Paris went in fear of her. She featured in many a music hall song of the time, best known of which is:

Je suis Mamselle Fifi,
(The singer cracks an imaginary whip)
Fifi!
(The audience calls Fifi)
Tu l'as dit boufi!
Je vais vous fouetter
(The singer cracks the imaginary whip again)
Dans la Rue de la Paix!
Hey hey!
(The audience repeats Hey hey)

Accused of conspiracy in the cases of The Minced Chinaman at Maxims (1901) and the aforesaid Voodoo Reign of Terror (1902) the charges against her remained unproven. However, in 1903 she was convicted of being an accessory in the Rue De La Paix Garrottings and shipped to Devil's Island. She escaped in 1903. This last being of great interest to penal historians as it was the first case of cannibalisation of prison warders to effect an escape. Several others were party to the prison break and collectively they became known as 'Les Anthropopagiques'. She married in London, 1905 and travelled widely throughout the world.

Her beauty and talent gave her entree to the very pinnacle of society. The loss of a leg in 1929 was the beginning of her downfall.

SEE: *'Famous Trials of 1901'. Famous Trials of 1903'.* See also: *'La Grande Madame de la Demi-Monde'*— Raoul Boule. *'The Complete Book of Etiquette', 'Ffrench Cuisine', 'Floral Artistry', 'Cake Decoration', 'The Book of Household Management', 'How To Raise Your Child', 'With a Whip',* all by Lady Ffifi Ffrench.;

5. 'NANNY' at Maidelthorpe manor in 1900 was one Evelyn Bondage. G.A.F. was not to know that in October of that year she had already been missing from the Manor for over two months, having failed to return from her annual summer holiday by the seaside. In police reports concerning her

disappearance, Lieutenant French (one 'F', no relation) an eye witness, said: *'One minute she was standing on the Mole, the next she was swept away by a great wave. There was nothing I could do. I shall be haunted by it forever* (LYME REGIS POLICE ARCHIVES). It later transpired that she had been rescued by a passing Arab dhow manned by white slave traffickers on their way to Tangiers with a cargo of Irish colleens. After being passed in at auction on three separate occasions in Morocco, she was shipped as a goodwill gift to the Bey of Algiers, who sent her to the Pasha in Constantinople, who sent her to the Khedive in Egypt, who sent her on to the Khan of Samarkand, Uzbekistan. It was while she was on this last journey that she overheard a plot to assassinate her new owner and reported it to him on the occasion of their first meeting. She was rewarded with her freedom and the gift of a camel. She left, taking all his camels, his horses, his harem and his heroin and soon became the most powerful and feared white slave trafficker in the East. Amongst other things, she is credited with being the first person to introduce horse racing to Hong Kong. Caught gun-running in 1903, she escaped and stowed away on the *'Kwin Belong Soda Water'* (A Philip Burns vessel under the captaincy of William P. Green) bound for New Guinea. However, due to a navigational error their first landfall was San Francisco in America. Evelyn had her considerable fortune sewn into her bloomers and thus gained entry to San Francisco society. Her lively sense of humour is evidenced by the fact that she called her new establishment there *'Bloomer Deals'.* Legend has it that E.B. or 'Nanny' as she was known to one and all, was actually a transvestite (a claim given credence by the fact that she had been spurned by her Arabian captors. However, in fairness, it must be said that her formidable physique and lack of conventional beauty could also have been the cause, (confidentially in some of her photographs she does appear to have a heavy growth of beard). Whatever the truth of it, the blame or the credit for what San Francisco subsequently became can be laid at her door. Cartoons of the era depict her as a demented bearded despot, but after the disappearance of several cartoonists the newspapers changed their attitude. Her influence and power spread throughout the land and it was not until 1905, when she opened a *'Bloomer Deals'* in New York City and came up against the fearful 'Anthropopagiques' that fate intervened. From then on she became known as 'Evel Bondage'.

SEE: *'Nanny Goes To Morocco'*, *'Nanny Goes To Turkey'*, *'Nanny Goes To The Near East'*, *'Nanny Goes To The Far East'*, *'Nanny Goes To Sea'*, *'Nanny Goes To The New World'*, *'Nanny Takes Her Friends For A Ride'*—Evelyn Bondage. *'Plastered In Paradise'*—Captain William P. Green. *'The Story Behind The Story: The San Francisco Riots'*—Benjamin Hardy. *'The Mysterious Case of The Disappearing Cartoonists'*—Agatha Crutchley. *'Sin Francisco'*—Martin Plaise. *'The Bowery Bloodbath'*—Frederick

Bowler. *'Bloomer Deals: American Enterprise At Its Best'*—Joshua Bryant. *'How To Make You First Million', 'How To Make Your Second Million', 'How To Become A Multi-Millionaire', 'Alcatraz', 'Alcatraz: The Need For Reform', 'My Time In Politics'*, all by Evel Bondage. *'Graft And Corruption In Our Political System'*—Daniel Cooleridge.

LETTER DATED NOVEMBER. 1900.

1. It is worth noting that G.A.F. has still not been informed of Nanny's disappearance.

THESE LETTERS WERE TRANSCRIBED
FROM THE ORIGINAL FFRENCH USING
A BROTHER C 70 TYPEWRITER
AND REPRODUCED ON
STRATAKOLOUR SUPPLIED BY
WIGGINS TEAPE